Free Yourself from Your Past – The 12-Day Workbook

By Derek Draper

Edited by Elloa Atkinson
(includes some original material by Dr. Cecilia d'Felice)

ISBN: 978-1723336584

PART ONE: YOUR JOURNEY

INTRODUCTION

Why – and how – does the past matter?

The past can be a strong platform on which you stand to confidently face the future, or a prison from which you feel you can never escape. Most people's histories are made up of both experiences which help them grow and experiences which have the potential to hold them back. Whatever the mix has been on your own life journey, I believe that you can't really understand where you are going if you don't understand where you've come from. That is what this 12-day workbook is designed to help you do. The intention isn't to wallow in the past, but to examine it so you can gain insights that allow you to resist repeating past mistakes and make the most of your potential in the future.

Maybe your career, your friendships, your relationship or your whole way of life seem stuck. It doesn't have to be like this. You don't have to let your past determine the way you feel now and what happens next. If you sense that old ways of thinking, feeling and acting might be limiting your ability to live life to the full, spend the next 12 days with me to focus on breaking free from the historic chains that have been weighing you down, celebrating the best of what has happened to you and, crucially, learning from both.

First though, some clarification. If you think you've heard conflicting messages about this issue, you'd be right. On one side are those who believe that the only way to move on in life is to analyse where we have come from and repair the ensuing damage. In vociferous opposition are those who insist such "naval gazing" is counterproductive: we just need to "let go" and embrace the future without so much as a backward glance, they argue. This dichotomy is reflected not only on the self-help shelves of your local bookshop but also in the loftiest academic debates on psychology. The debate entirely misses the point; worse, it tends to distract us, often leaving us doing nothing. The issue isn't whether we dwell on or disavow the past, as if either would ever be completely possible. Instead the key lies in the quality of our relationship to our past:

Are we at peace with our past or are we fighting it?
Do we accept our past is part of who we are, or do we
want to pretend it never happened?
Do we think that we are prisoners of our past, or can
we, in our present and future, rise above whatever has
happened?

This workbook will help you to answer these questions in a way that allows you to move on from your past rather than allowing it to control you. There are 12 exercises, designed to be tackled over 12 separate days, which I urge you to take your time over as you complete them. The exercises contain techniques that encourage you to think in different ways, but they won't work if you just skim read them and think, "Yeah, I get that". Intellectual understanding isn't enough. You need to experience each stage to let the lessons sink in. The emotions need to be surfaced and felt, however difficult that may be, before you can move on.

Our past experiences condition who and how we are today. Particularly when we were very young, other people's voices and actions entered our minds and determined what we expected the world to be like and how we expected to be treated by people. For this reason, let's assume that your parents or primary caregivers will be a key influence we will be examining over the next 12 days – although it could also be brothers, sisters, other relatives, friends and school mates. This cacophony of voices intermeshes with our own inbuilt genetic character to lay down a script, complete with stage directions, that has coloured our lives ever since. This internal script attempts to answer some of the most fundamental questions that determine the quality of our psychological lives, such as:

Do I feel safe? Taken care of?
Are people interested in me? Do they respect me? Do
they like me?
Will someone be there for me and have my best
interests at heart?

Am I a good person? Am I basically OK, or am I bad, evil or flawed?

If the messages we received in childhood were negative and undermining, we may have low expectations of ourselves or others, poor self-esteem and be guarded against intimacy. We need to recognise that these are the functions of what we were told, by word and deed, long ago. If we can decouple ourselves from these historic scripts, it is possible to develop new ways of feeling, thinking and being in the world.

This workbook breaks down a coherent programme of self-examination and development into twelve exercises to be tackled over a minimum of twelve days. Some will take up an hour or two; others will seem to be much shorter. Follow the timetable carefully. Once you have finished the day's task, spend additional time reflecting on it and perhaps revisiting it. Carve out space to allow insights and feelings to spring up and sink in.

Most of the exercises involve writing which is why the second part of the book is a journal. This will give you somewhere to make a record of this 12-day journey and can be something you can return to as you continue to learn and grow. It will capture the story of your life – not a life you have been condemned to live, but a life you can now begin to enjoy, free of the past.

Here's what we'll be covering over the next twelve days:

Day 1: Meet your internal critic
Day 2: Develop your internal ally
Day 3: Find your positive mantra
Day 4: Explore how were you parented
Day 5: Get in touch with your past selves
Day 6: Write your "three generation" letters
Day 7: Express your anger
Day 8: Identify your family's emotional dynamics
Day 9: Acknowledge your losses
Day 10: Remember compassionately
Day 11: Accept radically
Day 12: Let go

Obviously examining the past in this way has the potential to be distressing. If you feel too upset by this work, and especially if you suffered serious physical, emotional or sexual trauma as a child, or begin to believe you might have, I urge you to contact a mental health professional for support and guidance. You may also feel that this work is best done alongside seeing a therapist. I agree that is ideal, but I also know that many people have found this kind of work very beneficial in itself. Listen to and trust yourself as you navigate this material. When you're ready to begin, let's go.

Day 1: Meet your internal critic

We all have an internal critic – a narrator of sorts who passes judgement on who we are and how we live. This part of us is hostile and undermining. It critiques us as we go about our day like an arrogant talent show judge pulling apart someone's performance. To the critic, nothing we say or do is quite right. Our behaviour, mannerisms, personality and shortcomings (and for some people, even our strengths) all provide ample fuel for the internal critic's fire. We are, the internal critic says, too much and not enough – often at the same time.

Today, you are going to dive straight into the process of breaking free of this by meeting your internal critic and identifying exactly what it says about you. You're going to spend the day paying attention to all of the self-critical thoughts and half-thoughts that flit across your mind every day – even if they seem light-hearted or humorous. Some people find this easy to do, as their internal critic is extremely loud and easy to spot; for others, it's subtler – particularly for those of us whose internal critic usually directs its attention towards others. If you identify with the latter kind of person, remember that behind every critical thought about someone or something else, there usually lurks a criticism of self. Identifying that criticism is what you are aiming for today. If you catch yourself criticising others, pause and ask yourself what you are thinking or feeling towards yourself in that moment.

Simply reflecting on the internal critic is powerful enough, but you're going to take an extra step to help make this process as clear as possible: writing down the criticisms and identifying exactly what happened to trigger the thought in your journal at the back of this workbook. As you go about your day, pay attention to the moments when that inner voice criticises, attacks, judges or shames you – including the moments when you put yourself down out loud. For now, leave the third column blank. I've added some examples to give you an idea of what to look for.

What happened?	What does your internal critic say?	Leave blank for now
I dropped my phone and the screen smashed	I'm an idiot	
My boss asked me to correct a mistake	Why do I always get it wrong?	
I didn't get everything done that I needed to do today	I'm so useless and lazy	

Now put this part of the workbook aside and spend the next 24 hours reflecting, noticing and capturing your thoughts about yourself. I know it's tempting to read further but these exercises only work if you do them in the right order, at the right time. Come back once you have spent a day with this activity, and good luck.

Day 2: Develop your ally

Welcome back. If you spent yesterday paying attention to and noting down your critical thoughts, by now you might have a fairly long list in your journal. It can be sobering to see them in black and white, can't it?

If something went particularly badly yesterday, it was probably easy to identify what the internal critic was saying to you. If nothing out of the ordinary happened – just the stuff of normal life – the criticisms you noted down will still be representative of the kind of thoughts you have about yourself on any given day. You might have noticed that you repeatedly had the same critical thoughts over and over again. This is the case for a lot of people. However, it is also possible that your self-critical thoughts seem somewhat random and disparate, or you might have only identified two or three moments in the day where you criticised yourself. Whatever the case is for you, doing yesterday's exercise will have surfaced thoughts that you have about yourself and will give you a window into a concept I call Core Pathogenic Beliefs, or CPBs.

Core Pathogenic Beliefs are inaccurate and harmful beliefs or assumptions a person forms about themselves (hence calling them pathogenic – or diseased), usually early on in life, which over time become an internal script. The internal critic then spends years or decades drumming these in. For more information about CPBs and how they can affect you, see my book, *Create Space: How to Manage Time and Find Focus, Productivity and Success.*

There is both bad and good news when it comes to CPBs. The bad news is that every time your mind goes down one of these well-trodden paths of self-judgement – anytime you think a self-critical thought – you carve that mental pathway ever deeper, laying down and reinforcing neural pathways that become "undermining superhighways" in your brain's chemical make-up.

The good news is that when you can catch yourself doing this, stop it and consciously put a different thought in place, you begin to lay down new, alternative neural pathways that are more supportive, encouraging and generous. Though the mind can seem extremely stuck in certain patterns, the good news is that it can change. Over time, these new pathways run smooth and deep, and your old negative routes become metaphorically overgrown through disuse. This takes a significant amount of practice, but it is possible. It is like learning your times tables, a foreign language or riding a bike: *knowing* how to do it isn't the point. You need to practice it until it become an instinct, until, as with a regular yoga practice, your muscles become used to their new activity, literally changing shape and form. This happens through repetition.

The first step in countering your critic is to challenge each and every criticism by taking up a different perspective on what happened. In other words, you're going to cultivate the voice of your internal ally – the figurative "good twin" to your internal critic. Today you're going to develop the voice of your ally so that when the critic speaks (and it frequently will), you can counteract it with a different way of seeing yourself. To do this, you're going to get out the list you made yesterday and fill in the third column, which you'll remember you left blank. Carve out some quiet time and go through each and every criticism you captured yesterday; your task is to now write down what a kind, supportive friend would say to you about what happened. Another way of doing this is to imagine what *you* would say to a friend who was in the same position.

What happened?	What does your internal critic say?	What could your internal ally say?
I dropped my phone and the screen smashed	I'm an idiot	This doesn't happen often. It was a moment of lapsed concentration, that's all.
My boss asked me to correct a mistake	Why do I always get it wrong?	This is the first time in ages she's had a complaint and it's helpful to get feedback. Yesterday she came and praised me for that other project.
I didn't get everything done that I needed to do today	I'm so useless and lazy	You're not useless. You simply overestimated what you could get done. Next time, simplify and only put one to three key priorities into a work day.

You'll see from the examples above that the ally's voice doesn't need to be sugary sweet or over-exaggerated. It is important that it feels genuine to how *you* would speak to another person; if that means downplaying the positivity or being quite pragmatic, so be it. Equally, if what you are craving is affirmation and reassurance, then let the voice of the internal ally speak in that way. Beginning the work of cultivating the internal ally's voice can feel awkward and uncomfortable, because we are often so used to thinking critical thoughts that anything else feels fake or forced. The truth however is that what the internal ally has to say is actually far more honest and grounded in reality than the inner critic: not getting your tasks finished does not mean that you are lazy and useless as a human being. Usually, it simply means that you didn't prioritise as effectively as you could have. If over time, the same thing keeps happening, it still doesn't mean you're useless and lazy; it probably just means that you could learn some strategies for working more efficiently. And if you *are* being deliberately lazy in your work, my hunch would be that something's underlying that – perhaps you're not stimulated by your job, or perhaps, as if often the case, you are on a mission to prove to yourself and others that you are no good.

When you do today's exercise, make sure you go through all the thoughts you captured yesterday. If you had a long list, this might take a while and could feel tedious or challenging. Do it anyway; it will give you good practice and in catching the self-critical thoughts and challenging them.

In your day to day life, it is unlikely that you will catch every single self-critical thought you have. You will be busy or distracted, and sometimes you'll simply miss them because you are so used to thinking this way. Commit to catching and reversing the thoughts as often as you can. Don't just "think" the ally's response: *write it down*. This will help you get used to these new ideas, although they will feel unreal and uncomfortable for a while. Remember that a foreign language also feels awkward when you first start speaking it.

Day 3: Find your positive mantra

There is almost always a clear pattern in people's CPBs. Today you are going to continue strengthening the voice of the internal ally by developing an all-encompassing "umbrella" mantra: an intentional thought you can repeatedly think to challenge and counteract the core critical belief, in order to develop a new, healthy one.

If you haven't already done so, make sure you work out what your primary theme is. This will probably be obvious, but if it isn't, pick one self-judgement that seems to stand out and work on that. You can work on the others later. Here are three common examples:

I'm not good enough.
I always get it wrong.
I am useless.

Your task today is to create a mantra to tackle the CPB. Here are some suggested positive mantras to counteract the example CPBs I just listed:

I'm not good enough	*I am good enough, and sometimes I can be great!*
I always get it wrong	*I'm fallible like everyone, but I often get things right, and that makes me feel good.*
I am useless	*I sometimes need to work harder but I am proud of what I do well.*

I am conscious that these mantras may sound cheesy and "American", but I don't care. These are your positive affirmations, and you have a right to believe them about yourself. In fact, you will see that the mantras are not sugar-coated or hyperbolic. They acknowledge your imperfect human nature and are actually far more accurate than the sweeping self-critical generalisations that have maybe been dominating your internal dialogue for years.

Far from being ashamed of this new thought, I want you to celebrate it. Print it out on your computer in big colourful letters or put it onto Post Its and stick them around the house; take a Saturday afternoon to do something arty and creative that illustrates this new mantra; set an alarm on your phone to go off a few times a day to prompt you to remind yourself of it. You could even make it your screensaver! Don't shy away from this new thought: embrace it and dare to imagine what life would be like it you believed it. The goal today is to begin the process of integrating this thought into your psychological make-up. After all, you have probably spent years holding the critical version close to your heart without any hesitation at all. Be as welcoming to the positive replacement.

Day 4: Explore how were you parented

Now that you've addressed your internal critic and have found and strengthened the voice of your internal ally, it's time to begin looking to the past so that you can free yourself from it.

It is often agreed that being a parent is the most challenging and difficult of roles, one for which many are unprepared and unskilled. Despite our parents' best intentions, they sometimes got things emotionally wrong – often as a result of the way in which *they* were parented. Some parents are emotionally withdrawn, unable to meet the needs of their developing child. Some are neglectful, absorbed in their own worlds, forgetting there is someone they have given life to who needs their attention in order to grow and thrive. Some are emotionally explosive, controlling all the emotions in the family by taking total ownership of them, or who emotionally blow hot or cold, seemingly at random, making their children feel confused and anxious. There will also be those of us who will have experienced cruel, sadistic and abusive upbringings; these can be the most difficult to understand, work through and let go of. It is very important that when you try these exercises, you are gentle with yourself. Remember that exploring your past will create emotional demands on you and bring up memories that might be painful and disturbing. If you find that you are struggling, getting upset or becoming angry, take time out to reflect and remind yourself that it is normal to become distressed when revisiting these emotionally turbulent times and that your priority is to compassionately take care of your feelings. If things get too intense, as I said earlier, turn to a professional for support – a counsellor or psychotherapist.

Today's exercise is designed to help you make contact with the emotional reality of your past experience, for better or worse. Don't rush into this; take your time and ask yourself whether you feel ready to commit to this work as it may well be painful. If you do decide to commit to the exercise, take it slowly and gently. Take a pen and paper and ask yourself this question:

In this moment, do I feel some unhappiness with the way I was raised?

Focus individually on your mother, father and/or primary caregiver(s), asking yourself the question for each one. This can include grandparents, uncles and aunts, teachers or other significant adults in your childhood. If the answer is "Yes, I am unhappy", take a moment to reflect and then ask yourself the following questions, writing down your responses.

Did I feel loved by my mother, father and/or caregiver as a child? If I did feel loved, what form did this love take? If or when I did not feel loved, what form did the lack of love take?

Do I feel unhappy with the way my mother, father and/or caregiver expressed their love? If I feel unhappy, what is it about the way love was expressed (or not expressed) that I am unhappy about?

Work through the questions for each parent or caregiver individually.

You might want to explore whether you felt your parents' or caregivers' love was conditional, rigid, rule bound, constraining, emotionally distant, cold or bound by unreasonable expectations and demands.

Think about the messages that you repeatedly received from your parents or caregivers. Were they positive or negative? Did you feel accepted or judged? Write about your feelings, whatever they might be – sadness, distress, anger or pain – which are provoked by acknowledging the reality of your childhood experience.

Do not edit or judge yourself. The point of this process is to let out the feelings that you have probably tried to ignore, avoid or deny. You might well feel flooded with emotions when you finish this exercise. If you begin to feel overwhelmed, stop the exercise and do something that will nurture you and take care of your feelings: a walk, a call to a friend, or a hug from a loved one. Let the emotions out rather than trying to swallow or bury them. Crying can feel extremely painful but it is nature's inbuilt release system for dispelling and releasing pain. Return to the exercise only when you feel you have the emotional resources to continue.

Once you have completed this first exercise, review what you have written and monitor your feelings. Having written it down, what does it feel like to bear witness to your emotional truth? Capture these feelings on paper. If at this point you feel angry with your parents (and if and when you feel ready), tomorrow you might want to move on to the next exercise. If you don't feel ready, take a break for a few days and return when you feel able to continue.

Day 5: Get in touch with your past selves

The next exercise is a visualisation that allows you to meet and converse with the younger part of you that first experienced what you explored in day four. This is the self that first began to believe and internalise the criticisms and messages from your parents, caregivers or other influential people in your life. The intention today is to learn more about that more childlike part of you and start to let your stronger, adult self (the one who thinks like your ally and not your critic) to communicate with, and give comfort to this damaged part of you. This may sound weird or wacky, but suspend any disbelief; I have seen this exercise work time and time again, and most people get something very rich from it.

Step 1: Get ready

Find a quiet place and make sure you won't be interrupted by other people. Put your phone onto flight mode. Sit upright on a comfortable easy chair or sofa and close your eyes. Let your hands fall into your lap. Take deep breaths all the way into your abdomen, allowing your stomach to become full and round with each inhale. When you exhale allow a different part of your body to completely relax with each exhalation. Start with the top of your head, then your shoulders, upper arms, lower arms and hands, chest, stomach, legs, and finally your feet. Let yourself sink into the chair and the ground beneath you. You will feel relaxed. If thoughts enter your mind, imagine them as clouds floating across a blue sky. Watch them as they move through.

Step 2: Meet your past self

Begin to focus on the long list of critical thoughts that you uncovered in exercise one. Think about when you first started to hear and believe such things. How old were you? Conjure up a mental image of yourself at that age, and notice if you see yourself as very young, or primary school age, or a teenager. If it helps, let yourself see your clothes, environment and body language. See if you can gauge the expression on this "inner child's" face. Are you happy? Afraid? Excited? Something else?

Now begin to talk to this young part of you, from the loving adult part of yourself. Say whatever comes into your mind. It might be something like:

Hello, there? How are you? How are you feeling? What's going on for you, little one?

See what the child says in response. Your younger self may be shy, or withdrawn, or untrusting. You could say something back such as:

I know what you're feeling, because I feel like that too. I promise you though that it's not true. It's easy to believe the bad thoughts about ourselves but I'm here with you now and I'm going to do everything I can to help you.

As I've already said, there is no script for you to follow here. This is a chance to see what comes from this older, deeper, wiser, loving part of you. You may find that you don't get much out of the exercise, or you might get some amazing insights into what you've been feeling. The important thing is that you establish a link with this inner child, and convey that you are now going to work on being his or her ally, not yet another of the critics.

It may be that you feel the need to do this exercise more than once, with different "inner children" at different ages. Perhaps you want to meet and talk to the four-year-old who felt abandoned when Dad left home... the eight-year-old who felt shut out of Mum's happy new marriage... the twelve-year-old confused by puberty... the teenager feeling unpopular and picked on at school... don't judge yourself here. Just trust whatever comes up and follow it.

If you do want to work with multiple inner children, I suggest spreading the work out over a number of days. Take it a step at a time. There is no rush. Really give yourself permission to get to know this buried part of you. Start a relationship with him or her, nurture it, and watch it grow.

Day 6: Write your "three generation" letters

This exercise is a more formal way of continuing the work you did on day five with your inner child. This time you are going to write three letters. Again, I urge you not to just mull over doing this but to actually get out the pen and paper or sit at a keyboard and type. The three letters are:

1. From your inner child to you.
2. From your inner child to your parents (or the person you feel they need to communicate with. It could be another relative or a bully at school, for example.)
3. From you (as an adult) to your inner child.

The purpose of the second letter is to open up your thoughts and feelings; you will <u>not</u> be sending it to anyone, so feel free to express everything that is on your mind. Don't censor yourself. At some stage, you may choose to discuss some of what you learn from these exercises with others, but this is something you can do later, if at all.

You don't have to achieve a particular outcome with these letters. Everyone's process will be different. Some people write very detailed, long, letters; others write just a few words. Write whatever is true for you at this time. Here are some examples of what others have written.

From your inner child to you

I feel so lonely... I always felt like a failure... What's wrong with me?... Why do I feel so different?... I didn't feel loved... I don't know what to do... I'm so angry at the world but I've never been allowed to show it... I wonder if you will be there for me, or if you will let me down too...

From your inner child to your parents

Why did you treat me like this?... I needed more from you... It's so unfair... I didn't ask to be born!... I don't feel like I'm allowed to be angry at you... I don't understand why you did this... Couldn't you have stayed together for my sake?... I never felt like you listened... I tried so hard and you didn't seem to see it...

From you to your inner child

I understand you... I'm here... I'm not going anywhere... I am really going to try and change things... I know you're suspicious, I will do my best to help you trust me... I can see how much you are hurting, and how much you have always hurt... I can see your good side ... I'm going to show you how interested I am in you, and help you, and learn to love you...

Instead of pushing your hurt or emotions away, you can now choose to embrace them. This might sound strange: why would anyone actively choose to embrace something so painful? It can be helpful to imagine your distressed feelings as someone knocking on your door asking for help. If that happened, would you turn that person away, or would you let them in and try to comfort and take care of them? Probably the latter. This is what it means to embrace your pain, and this is what you're doing today.

Day 7: Express your anger

Looking at your past will almost inevitably bring up some anger. Feeling angry towards your parents is often uncomfortable, especially if you were raised in a home that was conflict averse or where your parents were not emotionally responsible, but I want to assure you that feeling anger is part of the process. Today's exercise is designed to help you work through any anger you feel towards your parents in a healthy and constructive way.

Turn to your Journal at the back of the book and write "I'm angry because" at the top of the page. Let yourself write anything and everything that comes to mind. I urge you not to censor yourself here but to try to let your pen move across the page freely. Don't plan or overly think about what comes up: just write.

As you write, you might want to think about particular events or times from your childhood when you felt angry with your parents or caregivers, regardless of whether you were able to express this at the time or not. Notice the quality of the feelings, where they are located in your body and whether they were acknowledged or taken care of at the time. Perhaps you were a child who was not allowed to express anger. Write down how this felt both when you were a child and now as an adult.

Some people like to go a bit further and get physical. Not many of us have a punching bag but you might want to find a place you can stomp around a bit, and or yell. Even cream. You could incorporate this energy into a strenuous work out at the gym. On the Hoffman Process, a residential therapy course, people are encouraged to get a big pillow and punch it, or hit it with a baseball bat. Just sitting on your bad and banging your fists on the mattress could allow some of your anger to be expressed and released.

Again, if you feel overwhelmed, take time out to reflect and recover, returning to the exercise only when you feel you are emotionally ready to.

Day 8: Identify your family's emotional dynamics

The previous exercises have been designed to put you in touch with your feelings about the way in which you were parented. You have explored, acknowledged and been truthful about how you felt as a child and how you feel now about your childhood. The next stage in this transformative process is to try and understand your parents' internal emotional world. This won't be easy, because when most of us think about our parents, it is often from a regressive childlike position, in which we feel hurt, rejected and misunderstood. It can be very easy to project these feelings into our parents and not to be able to see them objectively. If, however, we are to truly break free from our past, we need to find a more expansive way of understanding what happened to us, and this means trying to understand our parents and what might have happened to their emotional development. Again, this won't be easy, so go gently and if it feels too painful and difficult, take time away from this work and return to it only when you feel ready.

This exercise is to help you explore and understand how your parents expressed themselves emotionally. The way they communicated emotions to themselves, each other and to you will have had a direct impact on the way you felt (and feel) about yourself. Think and journal about the following questions:

How did my parents/caregivers express themselves emotionally?

Which emotions were expressed? Was there more emphasis on 'positive' emotions or 'negative' ones? Were some emotions more permitted than others?

Did my parents/caregiver 'sit on' their feelings, expressing very little? Did I learn that it was not 'nice', 'right' or 'appropriate' to express feelings?

Did one parent carry all the emotions in the family, to the exclusion of other family members' emotional expression?

Can I think of reasons why my caregivers might have expressed or not expressed themselves in this way?

Can I see whether my parents had emotional difficulties, issues or problems in relating to themselves, their partner and their children that would have been hard to understand as a child, but which become more accessible now that I am an adult?

Once you have explored how your parents expressed themselves emotionally, consider how you feel about them now. Review what you have written and compare your feelings with that of the anger exercise. See if you feel any differently now about your experience, however subtle that shift might be. Note this down, again identifying any shifts in affect, flashes of insight or understanding you might have gained today.

Day 9: Acknowledge your loss

Today's exercise is designed to help you reframe your childhood experience by acknowledging the losses that you faced as a child in the way in which you were parented, whilst also affirming to yourself as an adult your personal growth and development. Losses are a universal and unavoidable part of the human experience, but they often go unacknowledged, particularly if as children most or all of our material needs were met. If we had food in our bellies, clothes on our bodies and relative stability and security, it can be hard to acknowledge that we experienced certain emotional or psychological losses. Yet voicing the losses we experienced can be hugely liberating. It doesn't change what happened, but it can act as an emotional release valve, allowing us to look back and hold the beauty and the pain simultaneously.

Today you're going to explore the losses and the growth available to us as adults by working once again with affirmations. In her book *Self-Nurture: Learning to Care for Yourself as Effectively as You Care for Everyone Else,* Dr Alice Domar recommends internalising the following statements, either through meditation or as positive affirmations. Read through them and see which ones speak to you.

You gave me life, but I don't owe you my life.
I deserve to care for myself.
I have a right to your unconditional respect and care.
I won't live to prove myself to you.
It's never going to be perfect.
Separate, satisfied, serene.
I don't have to live out your unfulfilled dreams.
I am nourished by your love, despite your limitations.

These statements can point to the losses that you feel in your relationship with your caregivers as well as to the gains you have made as an adult living your own life. They are bittersweet yet also represent freedom from the past by acknowledging and accepting your emotional truth. Spend the rest of today working with these mantras. Tomorrow's exercise is about acceptance, which is the first step to letting go.

Day 10: Remember compassionately

It's easy to find ourselves endlessly ruminating on painful memories from the past. These ruminations can leave us feeling empty, sad, tearful and distressed as we go over and over the painful events, experiences and words that were spoken which hurt us.

Over the last ten days, you have been opening up your experience in a direct and explicit way. Through writing down your feelings, you have worked to acknowledge your past and your emotional truth in a powerful way. Your task now is to shift gears out of helplessly reliving your old pain and into taking care of yourself and practising self-compassion.

Staying trapped in a repetitious past does not help you grow emotionally. Instead of endlessly going round the same old loop, you can now begin to watch your memories arise, acknowledge them and then let them go. This will bring you closer to accepting your past which will free you to step fully into your present. By bearing witness to painful events, you can remind yourself that these things happened in the past, when you were very young, powerless and without a voice. As an adult, you are no longer small and powerless. Now, you *do* have a voice. The voice you can now choose for yourself is the voice of care and compassion, which can free you from the negative aspects of your past experience. (I recommend checking out Dr Kristen Neff's online quiz on self-compassion, which can help you identify clear ways in which you can begin to treat yourself more compassionately.)

Today, if you notice yourself revisiting past painful experiences, remind yourself that these are simply old memories. Instead of spiralling into feeling helpless and hopeless or into self-criticism, practise bearing witness to your process with compassion. Anytime you catch yourself thinking about your past or criticising yourself, imagine yourself as a loving parent whose sole focus is on providing care, love and support to a hurting child. Every time you do this, you deepen the work you did at the beginning of this process when you first found your internal ally.

Over time, responding to your thoughts, memories and emotions with compassion will help you become your own best friend.

Day 11: Accept radically

Today we are addressing two very powerful and challenging concepts: acceptance and forgiveness. Over the last 10 days you have been forging a different kind of path, one in which you looked honestly at what happened to you, acknowledged how you felt and feel, and identified what you made it mean about yourself. This process leads us naturally to the question of acceptance.

Sometimes in life we rush towards saying we've accepted the painful things that happened to us because we don't want to face, acknowledge and feel the truth of how we have been feeling. At other times, we cling onto the hurt and stubbornly refuse to accept what has been or to forgive because we fear that something will be lost somehow if we forgive. The truth however is that at a certain point, we have to face the challenge of accepting what we cannot change. What happened, happened. If we have faced and felt the pain, the next step is to address the question of how we are going to feel about our past going forward. Will we forgive, or will we continue to live in blame and resentment? Forgiveness creates acceptance, which in turn creates the possibility of being able to truly integrate what happened. This allows us to move forward without dragging our past into our present and future. We have to decide whether we are going to take emotional responsibility for ourselves from this point onward, or whether we are going to continue to wallow in the pain of what was done to us.

Real acceptance is not a passive resignation of what has gone before. It is a radical, assertive acknowledgement of our suffering and losses that simultaneously embraces our feelings with compassion. Acceptance alleviates the distress our history has caused us. With acceptance comes freedom: freedom from suffering, from our past, and from the Core Pathogenic Beliefs we have been carrying with us for many years and even decades. Acceptance allows us to step into the potential of our present moment and the possibility of a future free of unresolved emotional pain.

It might feel very hard to forgive your parents and caregivers for what happened in your childhood. This process doesn't happen in just one day, so have patience with yourself. You will cycle in and out of forgiveness many times, but the key is to stay aware of whether you are facing the right direction.

In this penultimate exercise, write your responses to the following questions:

What do I now believe about my past?

Can I accept what I believe about my past?

Can I let go of the hurt my past has caused me?

Can I let myself step into the present moment free of the hurt my past has caused me?

If you feel unable to set yourself free from the past after exploring today's questions, don't judge yourself. It may well be that you need more time to revisit some of the exercises and work through your feelings. You won't be alone if this is the case. A trusted friend or family member may be able to offer alternative perspectives and insights as to where and why you feel stuck.

Remember that you have carried these feelings for a lifetime, so they are not necessarily going to change immediately and there are some things that you might have to work through several times before you can come to a place of resolution. Be gentle with yourself, remind yourself that compassion for your feelings and for your experience is vital if you are to overcome the challenges of your early years and eventual freedom from your past. Hopefully, though, you will have made some solid progress during these 11 days of work and you can move on to the final exercise.

Day 12: Let go

As I said at the beginning of this workbook, being able to truly move on from your past requires a deep understanding of it. Only if you have made peace with who you are and how you became that way, only when you have acknowledged the pain you have been carrying, and only when you have worked to become your own friend instead of your enemy, can you really let go. If you don't do this, the negative effects of the past can lie deep within you, unacknowledged and corrosive, undermining your attempts to live a freer and more expansive life.

Ritual and ceremony have been part of our human lives since before the beginning of history and have persisted during all centuries, and in all cultures. I believe that this is because they provide powerful ways to symbolise and celebrate our achievements. Today, you are going to complete this process with a ceremony. I invite you to commit fully and embrace the spirit of this exercise. Don't fall at the last hurdle by getting shy. This exercise is designed to demonstrate symbolically that you have reached a point where you are letting go and moving on. You've already done the hard work required; your task now is to claim your right to let go and move on.

Design your own little ceremony. Some like to use a hot air balloon and let it go (others things this is not environmentally sound); others might build a little boat out of twigs and find a river, or drop a stone into a pond. You could light a small fire outside somewhere, or just use a trash can. Whatever means you use the idea is to send a message off somewhere – to let it go. So get a piece of paper and write down the essence of the inner critic's messages, which you discovered back in our very first exercise. Attach this to your balloon, little boat or stone, or get ready to crunch it up and burn it or simply throw it away. Don't get too self-conscious; people aren't going to be too interested in what you are up to. When you have found the right spot, take a few deep breaths. Conjure up the image of your inner child and say something along the lines of:

I'm doing this for you, for me and for us. We have been held back by these old messages from the past for too long. We have taken time together to explore this, and we have faced up to what happened. Now let's make a fresh start. Here is this negative rubbish, leaving us for ever...

Let go of whatever you have devised. Watch it disappear, taking with it those old, unhelpful, damaging messages that became part of you but which you have now broken free of. Visualise your inner child. I bet you anything he or she is smiling back at you.

To close the ceremony, visualise giving your little one a great big hug. Take him or her into your heart and imagine a special space to relax and play. You can always meet again in your imagination. You can take comfort from each other anytime you want or need to in the future.

In Closing

Over the last 12 days (or however long you have spent taking this journey), you have gone where many fear to tread. I do not say this lightly: facing up to the truth of your childhood experiences is often a painful process, and many people avoid it for years, even decades and, all too often, forever. It is, however, an unavoidable assignment if you want to live a life in which you genuinely transcend rather than just bury and ignore the impact of your childhood and formative experiences. Doing this takes work, as you know from personal experience!

In identifying the core pathogenic beliefs you have lived by, owning your anger, losses and pain, and in taking emotional responsibility, you have laid a sturdy foundation from which you can go forward into your life, no longer a prisoner of your past and neither cut off from it. Instead, you are in a position to remember the good times more easily; one benefit of facing and processing past trauma is the ability to recollect and integrate positive memories which will have been unintentionally blocked out when trying to suppress the bad ones. You may even be reading this now with a greater understanding and appreciation of everything you have lived through, knowing that however painful the bad times were, somehow, they helped you to become who you are today.

For now, our work is done. It is time to go home – to be at ease with the present, at peace with your past and looking forward to the future. Good luck.

PART TWO: YOUR JOURNAL

The following pages will offer you space to do each day's exercise, capturing your thoughts and feelings on paper. Use each part of the workbook in conjunction with the corresponding chapter from Part 1 of the book.

Day 1: Meet your internal critic and Day 2: Develop your internal ally

"Consistent positive self-talk is unquestionably one of the greatest gifts to one's subconscious mind."
— **Edmond Mbiaka**

What was happening?	What did your inner critic say?	What could your internal ally say?

What was happening?	What did your inner critic say?	What could your internal ally say?

Day 3: Find your positive mantra

"Words have a magical power. They can either bring the greatest happiness or the deepest despair."
— **Sigmund Freud**

Reflect on what this your own personal positive mantra might be, thinking back to the core pathogenic belief(s) that you have identified. Play with different ways of expressing your mantra and choose the one that feels right.

Day 4: Explore how were you parented

"The final forming of a person's character lies in their own hands."
— **Anne Frank**

Reflect on the following question:

In this moment do I feel unhappy with the way I was raised?

Focus individually on your mother, father and/or caregiver (which can include grandparents, uncles and aunts, teachers or other significant adults in your childhood), asking yourself the question for each. If the answer is 'yes', take a moment to reflect and then ask yourself the following questions, writing down your responses:

Did I feel loved by my mother, father and/or caregiver as a child?

If I did feel loved, what form did this love take and do I feel unhappy with the way my mother, father and/or caregiver expressed their love?

If I did not feel loved, what form did this unloving take?

Again, focus on each parent or caregiver individually.

46

Day 5: Get in touch with your past selves

"The most sophisticated people I know - inside they are all children."
— **Jim Henson**

What happened during my visualisation?
What do I think and feel about this?
What insights am I taking away?

Day 6: Write your "three generation" letters

"Your willingness to wrestle with your demons will cause the angels to sing."
— **August Wilson**

Write three letters:

1. From your inner child to you.
2. From your inner child to your parents (or the person you feel they need to communicate with. It could be another relative or a bully at school, for example).
3. From you (as an adult) to your inner child.

Letter 1: From your inner child to you

Letter 2: From your inner child to your parent(s)/caregiver(s)

Letter 3: From you (as an adult) to your inner child

Day 7: Express your anger

"There will be an end to your pain. And once you've released all those pent-up emotions, you will experience a lightness and buoyancy you haven't felt since you were a very young child."
— **Patricia Love**

Explore the following questions:

What form does anger towards my parents take?
What comes out of me if I think about this?
How might I release some of this negative energy?

Day 8: Identify your family's emotional dynamics

"Many of the habits of dysfunctional families use are not from the lack of love but are the result of fear. Knowing the love-limiting habits and behaviours of dysfunctional families is a wonderful beginning to lower the fear, allowing us to be real, allowing us all to learn how to love better."
— David W. Earle LPC

Explore the following questions:

How did my parents/caregiver express themselves emotionally?

Were only negative emotions expressed? Or were only positive emotions allowed to be expressed? How?

Did my parents/caregiver 'sit on' their feelings expressing very little? Did I learn that it was not 'nice', 'right' or 'appropriate' to express feelings?

Did one parent carry all the emotions in the family, to the exclusion of other family members' emotional expression? How did this manifest?

Can I think of reasons why my caregivers might have expressed or not expressed themselves in this way?

Can I see whether my parents had emotional difficulties, issues or problems in relating to themselves, their partner and their children that would have been hard to understand as a child, but become more accessible now that I am an adult?

Day 9: Acknowledge your losses

"All the art of living lies in a fine mingling of letting go and holding on."
— **Havelock Ellis**

What are my reflections about the loss I experienced when growing up?

Day 10: Remember compassionately

"Self-compassion is simply giving the same kindness to ourselves that we would give to others."
— **Christopher Germer**

Identify a past experience that you know you tend to ruminate on helplessly. Instead of going around the same old loop, today let the ally you discovered on Day 2 become a compassionate best friend who wants to help you see things differently.

Listen to the voice of your internal ally as it shows you a different way of seeing the situation. This is the compassionate part of you, the part that does not want to stay stuck remembering the past in a painful way.

Write down what your internal ally says about this past experience.

How do you feel after connecting with the voice of your internal ally?

Day 11: Accept radically

"Radical Acceptance is the willingness to experience ourselves and our lives as it is."
— **Tara Brach**

Explore the following questions:

What do I now believe about my past?
Can I accept what I believe about my past?
Can I let go of the hurt my past has caused me?
Can I let myself step into the present moment free of the hurt my past has caused me?

Day 12: Let go

"In the process of letting go you will lose many things from the past, but you will find yourself."
— **Deepak Chopra**

Explore the following questions:

What am I going to do to let go, and why?

Now go and do your ritual. Afterwards, come back and explore the questions on the next page.

How was the ritual for me?
How do I feel now?

The Rest of My Days

"I dwell in possibility..."
– **Emily Dickinson**

How do I plan to use what I have learned in these twelve days in all the days I have left to live?

RESOURCES AND FURTHER READING

Books

Create Space: How to Manage Time and Find Focus, Productivity and Success, Derek Draper
Self-Nurture: Learning to Care for Yourself as Effectively as You Care for Everyone Else, Alice Domar and Henry Dreher
You Can Change Your Life with the Hoffman Process, Tim Laurence
Overcoming Childhood Trauma: A Self-Help Guide Using Cognitive Behavioural Techniques, Helen Kennerley
The Drama of Being a Child and the Search for the True Self, Alice Miller
The Primal Wound, Ann Gila and John Firman
Self-Esteem, Matthew McKay and Peter Fanning
Self-Compassion Quiz by Kristin Neff (available online at self-compassion.org)

Websites

Derek Draper: https://derekdraper.net/
CDP Leadership Consultants: https://cdp.consulting/

Get in touch

Email: derek@cdp.consulting
LinkedIn: https://www.linkedin.com/in/derekdrapercdp/
Twitter: @derekdraper